STUDIES IN ENGLISH LITERATURE No. 1

General Editor
David Daiches
Dean of the School of English and American Studies
University of Sussex

MILTON: COMUS and SAMSON AGONISTES

by

J. B. BROADBENT

Fellow of King's College,
Cambridge

EDWARD ARNOLD (PUBLISHERS) LTD.

41 Maddox Street, London, W.1

First published 1961
Reprinted 1964, 1965

Printed in Great Britain by Richard Clay and Company, Ltd.,
Bungay, Suffolk

General Preface

It has become increasingly clear in recent years that what both the advanced Sixth Former and the university student need most by way of help in their literary studies are close critical analyses and evaluations of individual works. Generalisations about periods or authors, general chat about the Augustan Age or the Romantic Movement, have their uses; but often they provide merely the illusion of knowledge and understanding of literature. All too often students come up to the university under the impression that what is required of them in their English literature courses is the referring of particular works to the appropriate generalisations about the writer or his period. Without taking up the anti-historical position of some of the American 'New Critics', we can nevertheless recognise the need for critical studies that concentrate on the work of literary art rather than on its historical background or cultural environment.

The present series is therefore designed to provide studies of individual plays, novels and groups of poems and essays, which are known to be widely studied in Sixth Forms and in universities. The emphasis is on clarification and evaluation; biographical and historical facts, while they may, of course, be referred to as helpful to an understanding of particular elements in a writer's work, will be subordinated to critical discussion. What kind of work is this? What exactly goes on here? How good is this work, and why? These are the questions which each writer will try to answer.

DAVID DAICHES

Acknowledgement

The extract from *Burnt Norton* by T. S. Eliot on page 49 is reproduced by kind permission of Messrs. Faber and Faber.

Contents

COMUS

1. Introduction

Setting

About 1632, when Milton was a young graduate studying in a Buckinghamshire village, he was asked to write a masque for the dowager Countess of Derby. As the climax of this piece, *Arcades*, the Countess's grandchildren were ceremonially presented to her at her home, Harefield in Middlesex. Among the grandchildren probably taking part were Lady Alice Egerton, Lord Brackley and Thomas Brackley, children of the Earl of Bridgewater. He was the Countess's stepson and son-in-law and lived quite near, at Ashridge in Herts.

That was a simple family affair. A year or so later, though, the Earl of Bridgewater was made Lord President of Wales. To celebrate his installation at Ludlow in Shropshire a more elaborate masque was to be held, and the Earl's children presented to him. Milton was commissioned to write this too, and again the production was in the hands of Henry Lawes, music tutor to the Bridgewaters; he was a well-known court musician, the friend of Herrick and Waller and of Milton's father, also an accomplished musician.

So Milton, though a studious recluse, was in touch with the great houses of the provinces, and they with a great poet. They were minor courts, making their own clothes, educating their own children and nourishing their own cultural life. Their cultural relations were as closely woven as their blood-ties (see chart overleaf).

The two families were related by blood or patronage to Nashe, Greene, Ben Jonson, Marston; Spenser had written an elegy on the death of the Earl of Derby (a distant relative of his); the Countess's second husband, Sir Thomas Egerton, had employed Donne as secretary; the first recorded performance of *Othello* was at Harefield in honour of Queen Elizabeth; at Ludlow Sir Philip Sidney's sister, the Countess of Pembroke, had spent her childhood.

In such homes, and at the royal court, masque had begun in the sixteenth century as simple charades, and masked dances such as seen in Act V of *Love's Labour's Lost*. Later they added fancy dress to the masks, torchlight processions, and used masques to celebrate occasions, as in the

masque for a wedding (e.g. Jonson's *Masque of Hymen*) described in
L'Allegro:

> There let *Hymen* oft appear
> In Saffron robe, with Taper clear,
> And pomp, and feast, and revalry,
> With mask, and antique Pageantry ... (125)

Here would be set dances by the ladies, the courtiers, by professiona
morris dancers, and finally of the ladies and courtiers together. Some-

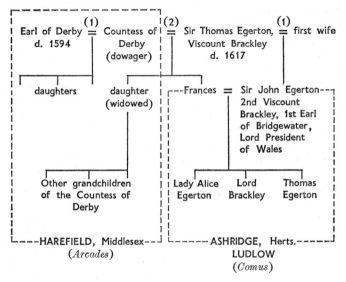

times the men would choose partners from the spectators, as in *Romeo
and Juliet*, I. v, and so implicate them in the little plot. In the seventeenth
century, at the more sophisticated courts of James I and Charles I, the
masque over-ripened. Masquers took the parts of pastoral, mythological
and allegorical characters, such as one meets in Spenser, although these
were fading from written literature; and while the serious, highly
verbal Morality play declined, its conflict between vices and virtues also
became the excuse-for-a-plot of frivolous and operatic masque. The
hub was still the courtly masked dance, but there were now also anti-
masques of bad, ludicrous or low-class characters; for, between the end
of the 'device' or plot and the epilogue or finale the masquers always

danced and feasted with the audience. The Brackley boys appeared in a masque like this earlier in the year of *Comus*. It was *Coelum Britannicum*, produced by the Inns of Court with the libretto by Carew (author of the famous elegy on Donne), the decor by Inigo Jones the architect and the music by Lawes. They put it on in Whitehall as a compliment to Charles I and Henrietta Maria, and as a satire on Puritan objections to the courtly extravagance and theatricals of which it is an example.

Into a fantastically elaborate scene descend Mercury, and Momus the god of fault-finding. They present, in parody, a cosmic reform—the vices, the figures of the zodiac and various animals dance anti-masques and are banished. Plutus, the god of materialism, introduces an anti-masque of country dancers, and Poenia, the goddess of poverty, one of gypsies; Fortune brings on a battle, and 'Hedonë, Pleasure, a young woman with a smiling face, in a light lascivious habit', calls up her 'subtle organs of delight', the five senses, who 'With changing figures please the curious eye, And charme the eare with moving harmony'. Mercury banishes her:

> Bewitching syren, guilded rottennesse,
> Thou hast with cunning artifice display'd
> Th'enamel'd outside, and the honied verge
> Of the faire cup, where deadly poyson lurks.
>
> .   .   .
>
> Griefe is the shadow waiting on thy steps,
>
> .   .   .
>
> Yet thy Cyrcean charmes transforme the world.

Here Momus goes off and Mercury presents the glory of Britain in various songs and scenes, including 'a troope of young lords and noblemens sonnes, bearing torches . . . apparelled after the old British fashion in white coats, embroydered with silver'. The masquers, having danced on the stage, descend and 'dance the revels with the ladies' in the audience, 'which continued a great part of the night' until the finale, in which Eternity celebrates the King and Queen as the consummation of all virtue.

This is an example of the over-ripe masque of later years. But even in its heyday the masque was frivolous. In Jonson's masque of *Pleasure Reconciled to Virtue* (1619) Comus is introduced as 'the Bouncing Belly, First father of sauce and deviser of jelly'; there are anti-masques of men in the shape of bottles, and of pigmies dancing round the sleeping

Hercules; the relationship between Pleasure and Virtue is not in any way dramatised.

Comus is a literary text of 'A Masque presented at Ludlow Castle 1634: On Michaelmasse night'; but even the shorter acting version was more dramatic, poetic, coherent and serious than any other masque, yet still fulfilling, with provincial economy and delicacy, the courtly occasion.

2. *Prologue*

Occasion

Michaelmas, 29 September, was the traditional day for electing magistrates and governors, so it was appropriate for installing the Earl of Bridgewater in what amounted to something like a vice-royalty. It is the feast of St. Michael and all angels, hence of guardian angels. The archangel Michael, captain of the heavenly host and conqueror of the dragon, was the medieval counterpart of Hermes-Mercury, messenger of the gods and a frequent introducer of masques; his special gift to men was prudence. The masque opens with the Attendant Spirit descending like Michael-Mercury from the sky to protect the temperance of the Lady and her brothers. In Milton's first draft he is called a daemon, that is in neo-Platonic mythology a tutelary spirit inhabiting a vague heaven where all souls go disembodied after death. Daemons had been identified with guardian angels, and the part was played here by Lawes, the children's tutor.

Spectacle

Nowadays *Comus* is quite often acted in the open air (e.g. at Regent's Park); but it was originally performed in the 30 × 60-foot hall of Ludlow Castle. Although as masques go it is not spectacular, the spatial relationships within it are important. The Spirit descends from on high to 'this pin-fold here', calling attention to the artificiality, the conventions, of his stage, as Shakespeare did to his 'wooden O'; and suggesting that on earth 'every man's a player' in a cosmic drama. Then Bacchus,

> Coasting the *Tyrrhene* shore, as the winds listed,
> On Circes Iland fell . . . (49)

The verb hints at the fall of Adam. Bacchus's son, Comus, stays horizontal, 'Roaving the *Celtick*, and *Iberian* fields'; and his aim is to degrade men from erectitude to bestiality. The final rescue of the Lady is effected by Sabrina rising from the nether region of waters. So the human characters, who keep glancing up at the stars, play their virtuous parts against the demi-godlike vice of Comus, who looks down to the animal; while beneficent powers help from above and below. The Elder Brother's hyperbole about the self-destructiveness of evil is justified by the masque's spatial framework:

> If this fail,
> The pillar'd firmament [sky] is rott'nness,
> And earths base built on stubble. (597)

You notice similar spatial patterning in all those painted vaults and *trompe l'œil* perspectives of baroque architecture; in less serious form it is characteristic of the later masque, dominated by scene-designers like Inigo Jones. It derives from the Ptolemaic scheme of the universe as a series of spheres, in which the stars, planets, sun and moon are embedded, revolving round the earth; from the Christian notion of a heaven above and a hell beneath; and from the period sense of architecture (more secular than in the Middle Ages—paid for by, so celebrating, a wealthy individual or class) as one of man's highest achievements. It models a reassuring cosmos. Of course, such a spatial scheme is too rigid for realism. We, having lost all three notions behind it, enact our realistic dramas in the closed square of living-room, cocktail-party, bed-sitter or backyard. Paradoxically, this is just as limiting: for the fullness of reality you need the ranging symbolic scenes of Lear's heath, the sea-coast of Bohemia, Brecht's Caucasian ravine.

Plot

The plot of *Comus* is of the unrealistic kind met nowadays in Westerns, science-fiction, comic opera, musicals. The good young girl is kidnapped and threatened with symbolic rape by the sophisticated gangleader, but remains defiantly inviolate; her elder brother is thoughtful and brave, the younger more practical and anxious. These are possible types of character, but the plot is unrealistic. The villain's assault, and the girl's resistance, are gestures: in a more realistic convention Tess of the d'Urbervilles, and Temple Drake in Faulkner's *Sanctuary*, are debauched, with a degree of willingness. The rescue, which we know will be in time, is effected by a fairy godfather and godmother—that is, by supernal power enlisted on the side of weak goodness against bad strength; here, a closer analogy is C. S. Lewis's *The Lion, the Witch and the Wardrobe*. The plot, then, presents in narrative form a rite whose purpose is to ward off evil by defining it, allowing it a limited token success and then defeating it by cosmic logic. One might suspect also that it allows us to enjoy sin in prospect and virtue in the event. Children make up fantasies like this, and popular national history is often based on them (e.g. *Joshua* and *Judges* and some English history books). Tragedy, even tragi-comedy, is superior because more real. Lear, after a world of evil, is rescued, but evil catches him up again. Perdita is found, but not until she, her father, mother, brother and her saviour Antigonus have suffered actual or symbolic death. The plot of *Comus*, then, appears in isolation as an example of the higher wishful-thinking. But it does not exist in isolation. The characters and their situation are actual. Possibly the children came from Ashridge to Ludlow later than their parents; anyway, the plot thickens when seen as a version of what was actually happening:

> And all this tract that fronts the falling Sun
> A noble Peer of mickle trust and power
> Has on his [Neptune's] charge, with temper'd awe to guide
> An old and haughty Nation proud in Arms;
> Where his fair off-spring, nurs't in Princely lore,
> Are coming to attend their Fathers state
> And new-entrusted Scepter, but their way
> Lies through the pérplex't paths of this drear Wood . . . (30)

The local, personal vibration, the sense of here-and-now this very day, make up for the deficiency of imagined drama.

Mythology

The Attendant Spirit sets the whole masque in a mythological context —'*Neptune* besides the sway Of every salt flood, and each ebbing stream . . .' (17). The Earl of Bridgewater becomes a vassal of Neptune, Comus in his Shropshire wood is the son of the ecstasy-provoking wine-god Bacchus, and of Circe who allured Odysseus. So Lady Alice and her brothers are acting in a divine drama, the struggle between good and evil, light and dark: 'We wrestle not against flesh and blood but against

principalities and powers, against spiritual wickedness in high places'
(*Eph.* vi. 12).

Much of the Spirit's prologue has the obvious adjectives and trite
insistent rhythms of pantomime:

> At last betakes him to this ominous Wood,
> And in thick shelter of black shades imbowr'd,
> Excells his Mother at her mighty Art,
> Offring to every weary Travailer,
> His orient liquor in a Crystal Glasse . . . (61)

and, repetitiously, to the Brothers:

> Within the navil of this hideous Wood,
> Immur'd in cypress shades a Sorcerer dwels
> Of *Bacchus*, and of *Circe* born, great *Comus*,
> Deep skill'd in all his mothers witcheries . . . (520)

It is partly that verse is here performing the routine informative func-
tion that prose was hardly fit for till the eighteenth century. But the
alliteration and the incantatory rhythm are also presenting the facts as
obviously mythological. Yet the Spirit insists that, if read properly, the
myth and allegory are 'true' in a special way—the 'psychological truth'
of a modern novel:

> for I will tell ye now
> What never yet was heard in Tale or Song
> From old, or modern Bard in Hall, or Bowr. (43)

> Ile tell ye, 'tis not vain, or fabulous,
> (Though so esteem'd by shallow ignorance)
> What the sage Poets, taught by th' heav'nly Muse,
> Storied of old in high immortal vers
> Of dire *Chimera's* and inchanted Iles,
> And rifted Rocks whose entrance leads to hell;
> For such there be, but unbelief is blind. (513)

Later, Milton said he dared to hold 'our sage and serious poet Spenser',
the arch-allegorist, 'a better teacher than Aquinas.' It is a rather crude
notion of how the insights of poetry work; but it fits masque. It is a
theme of this one.

Music

At each stage there is a 'Hark!' The Spirit hears 'the tread of hatefull steps' (91). The Lady enters saying, 'This way the noise was, if mine ear be true' (170). Sabrina is invoked to 'Listen and save'. At the centre of this motif is the Spirit's narrative of how his 'rural minstrelsie' was interrupted—

> The wonted roar was up amidst the Woods,
> And fill'd the Air with barbarous dissonance . . . (549)

That gave place to silence, and Silence was 'took ere she was ware' by the Lady's song, 'strains that might create a soul Under the ribs of Death' (561). The music essential to masque is being treated with Platonic seriousness. The action is a struggle between a discord which symbolises unregenerate nature and a harmony which is rational and of God.

3. *Comus*

Renaissance pictures show Comus as a Bacchus-like figure attending as master of the revels on courtly dances. But the Spirit has already shown he is a bad character. His badness has also been established by sight and sound: 'with him a rout of Monsters headed like sundry sorts o wilde Beasts, but otherwise like Men and Women, their Apparel glistring, they come in making a riotous and unruly noise, with Torches in their hands'. 'Oughly-headed monsters' are fearful no doubt for psychological reasons; they are abhorrent in Christian art because they recall the gods of Egypt (ultimately, the magical masks of prehistoric men as shown in the Lascaux murals). Here they are also on the wrong side by convention: they are the *anti*-masque.

Comus's first speech illustrates some of the functions of mythology in Renaissance poetry. It is a way of elaborating on nature which neither science nor Wordsworthian response to detail has superseded:

> And the gilded Car of Day,
> His glowing Axle doth allay
> In the steep *Atlantick* stream . . . (95)

This allusion to the sun-chariot of Helios–Phoebus–Apollo submerging in the earth's girdle of ocean is a way of saying not what a sunset is but what it looks like—the sun sizzling into the sea's horizon; and what it reminds us of—the steep roundness of the earth. It is also a way of making it happen, of enforcing sunset as a willed event in the action, in a way that a more naturalistic description would not do (this is why the invocation of Sabrina consists of classical allusions: she is being conjured by the authority of all the aquatic deities of Greece). In superbly enactual lines—

> The Sounds, and Seas with all their Finny drove
> Now to the Moon in wavering Morrice move,
> And on the Tawny Sands and Shelves,
> Trip the pert Fairies and the dapper Elves . . . (114)

—Comus justifies his riot by an appeal to nature, and nature deities: this anticipates his argument with the Lady. Then he accelerates from good cheer to lasciviousness. This change is implausible; but with the invocation of Cotyttyo he hints at witchcraft. The priest of a black sabbat was a man, to whom the female witches paid sexual reverence in their orgy. His rhythm reaches frenzied speed—

> Com, knit hands, and beat the ground,
> In a light fantastick round

—to start the anti-masque, and that no doubt was associated with witchcraft via country-dancing.

4. The Lady

Pastoral

The Lady thinks at first that Comus's revelry is a harvest-festival:

> me thought it was the sound
> Of Riot, and ill manag'd Merriment,
> Such as the jocond Flute, or gamesom Pipe
> Stirs up among the loose unleter'd Hinds,
> When for their teeming Flocks, and granges full
> In wanton dance they praise the bounteous *Pan*,
> And thank the gods amiss. [171]

This is uncomplimentary to the local villagers, who would just have been celebrating their harvest. Most pastoral is ambivalent about the country like this. To understand why, we have to consider pastoral as a literary form.

We all have regions of the mind in which we construct fantasies. But the serious imagination also seems to need, for certain purposes, a setting or environment free of the demands of realism. The setting itself need not be fantastic—indeed, it is bound to have a basis in reality; but it must allow things to happen which might be absurd in actual life or in a realistic story. Usually (as in comedy) the things that people are allowed to do, and the things fate arranges, fulfil common fantasies of power, love and so on, and ensure a happy ending. Every age has an unreal setting peculiar to its own interests—obviously, in the twentieth century cosmic space and future time form one. The country has always been used in this way, and such treatments of it are called 'pastoral' or bucolics or eclogues (though the characters may be ploughmen, and there have been 'piscatory eclogues' about fishermen). Now, writing about these escape-areas always implies a contrast between them and actuality; and it is the management of this contrast which can be so serious. In the case of pastoral the contrast is between urban life, with its hypocritical courtesy, its civilised sinfulness; and the rough goodheartedness, the 'natural' virtue, of rural life.

At the Renaissance the main literary escape-area was the classical world, and the classics had their own pastoral tradition. The chief Greek pastoral poems were by Theocritus, a poet of the third century B.C. who spent part of his life in metropolitan Alexandria but wrote about the shepherds of his native Sicily; the chief Latin ones were the *Eclogues* of Virgil. Theocritus's poetry is sophisticated and to a large extent it accorded with already-established conventions; but it did subsume a number of real country legends, superstitions, rites, and it is possible that the poems occasionally echo the speech of Sicilian shepherds. In the fields of third-century Sicily there survived an ancient culture based on the seasonal occasions of ploughing, sowing, harvest, sheep-shearing; the need to acknowledge and propitiate natural forces like rain and sun; the need, in the absence of fertilisers and veterinary medicine, to encourage crops by magic ('fertility rites'), and to make out of these activities some sort of religion and entertainment; so the local cults of nature gods and (especially) goddesses bore little relation to the official religion of the wider world, though that religion was paid lip-service to—the local thunder-god re-named Zeus, the local mother-goddess worshipped as Ceres (as, in parts of southern Italy, she is still worshipped as the Virgin Mary). Some of the rites would be frankly sexual; and that frank simplicity of country people, though refreshing to the jaded urban poet, could also be shocking. Hence Hamlet's pun on 'country matters': most pastoral poetry is about love. When the Renaissance poets took up pastoral they subsumed into the classical form English folklore; but because the Reformation was occurring simultaneously the inherent tension between rural simplicity and rural grossness was tightened. Hence the ambivalence.

So, the Lady's association of real evil, in the shape of Comus, with the loose morals and lingering paganism of peasants, links the masque's plot and characters with the pastoral convention and with the time of year; but it is also an example of the grudging, antiseptic kind of Puritanism which pulled down the maypoles, and which even now demolishes gas-lamps, winding streets, because they are untidy and 'medieval', and puts car-parks in their place. We're likely to prefer the wild wood to the asphalt jungle. Even the Renaissance Lady, mistaking Comus, does understand something of what may be good in country life:

> Shepherd I take thy word,
> And trust thy honest offer'd courtesie,
> Which oft is sooner found in lowly sheds
> With smoaky rafters, then in tapstry Halls
> And Courts of Princes, where it first was nam'd. (321)

But there is no genuine representative of country courtesy in the masque. There wasn't, usually, in pastoral literature generally: in Book VI of the *Faerie Queene* Sir Callidore, the knight of courtesy, finds a beautifully mannered girl in the country and woos her; but she turns out to be a foundling, and a princess by birth.

The same insistence on courtesy-by-blood is met in *Cymbeline*, and in the *Winter's Tale* where 'pastoral' takes on the force of 'paschal': the loving innocence of Perdita in the sheep-shearing scene 'redeems' her family and reconciles Sicilia with Bohemia. Between that and *Comus* is Fletcher's *Faithful Shepherdess*, a tragi-comedy first acted in 1608, the year Milton was born. Fletcher's verse influenced *Comus* a good deal; but Fletcher used the pastoral world much more than Milton to project patterns of actual (and plausibly sophisticated) behaviour; and, though Fletcher shared the Lady's anxiety about loose unlettered hinds, he tried

B

to make them good in the end. He did this by means of a virgin shepherdess, Clorin, mourning a lover who died before the play began.
Having sworn herself to chastity, she heals with herbs the other characters' love-wounds—that is, she imputes to their love the purity of her
chastity. For example, a pair of simply true lovers, Perigot and Amoret,
are thwarted by jealousy and black magic but reunited by Clorin in the
end. They are not pure like Clorin, though: it is because Amoret agrees
to sleep with Perigot that they get into difficulties—they have to learn
chastity. The play starts with a harvest festival, and most of the action
takes place at night, emphasising the invitation to, and injunction not to,
indulge in sex as a concomitant of natural fertility. It is in these terms
that Fletcher states Milton's theme, the use of nature: all, except the un-
naturally lustful but loveless Sullen Shepherd and the naturally neutral
Daphnis, do 'use' nature; all are hurt by using it wrongly, but healed by
Clorin and sent back to try again.

Fletcher is a psychologist; Milton, more a philosopher, takes an
arbitrary and rather puritanical attitude to his materials. The 'wild
Wood' in which the Lady finds herself is assumed to be wholly nasty—
'drear, ominous, tangled, Chaos, dungeon, hideous'. We are familiar
with this symbolism from *The Wind in the Willows*, and from Milton's
horrified fascination with 'the tangles of *Naeara's* hair'. The convention
is true of childhood fears; of the fear of madness, 'of calling shapes, and
beckoning shadows dire' (207), such as the Lady suffers; and fear of the
chaos into which society and individual fall when they lose fixed points
of reference, a sense of black and white. But, based on fear, it is a negative
convention; it assumes the superiority of what is rational and orderly to
what is more 'emotional' or 'natural'. The ideas behind the convention
are attacked by Romantic writers: 'Oh for a life of sensations rather
than thoughts' (Keats); Blake's *London* and *Garden of Love* condemn the
ordered structures; Lawrence demanded 'Chaos in Poetry'; Ibsen's
characters dash out of their bricked-up lives into the river, up the moun-
tain; Freud saw civilisation as the cause of all our discontents. Milton
was personally scared of the wild wood of passion, and the society of his
time had reason to be scared of political chaos. We are post-Romantics,
so we may not share Milton's feelings. Our anxiety is not so much that civil
war, rebellion, lust will well up from below and lose us in the wild
wood, as that reason will too reasonably frustrate our proper instincts,
and government impose chaos—the bomb, torture, tyranny—from
above.

But within his prejudices and his genre, Milton handles our problem. His wild wood gives place in the last scene to 'Ludlow Town and the Presidents Castle'; that suggests an unthinking preference for institutions, government, law, over the wild wood; but the presentation of Comus's home as 'a stately Palace' also, 'set out with all manner of deliciousness: soft Music, Tables spread with all dainties', shows that though Ludlow Castle may represent as absolutely good an orderliness which is only partially so, there is another even more questionable kind of order—ordered lust. The change of scene is from the certain tyranny of greed to the possible tyranny of reason: Mammon House versus the civil service.

Music of the Spheres

The most dramatic part of the Lady's first speech (lines 195b–225) was excluded from the production at Ludlow. It shows her appealing to the stars to give her light, where Comus, though an imitator of 'the Starry Quire', prayed for darkness to fall. She finds herself, shiveringly, where the noise came from; it is empty, but redolent of presences, and she sways into horror. But she remembers she is attended by Conscience, that 'strong siding champion' like one of Spenser's knights or Mr. Greatheart in the second part of *Pilgrim's Progress*; she sees Faith, Hope and the Platonic 'form' of Chastity; and her belief in the Attendant Spirit is justified by a crucial flicker of moonlight which she presents in a figure of speech:

> Was I deceiv'd, or did a sable cloud
> Turn forth her silver lining on the night?
> I did not err, there does a sable cloud
> Turn forth her silver lining on the night,
> And casts a gleam over this tufted Grove. (221)

So her spirits are 'new enliven'd' and she sings. Comus's compliment to the Lady's echo-song—

> Can any mortal mixture of Earth's mould
> Breathe such Divine inchanting ravishment? (244)

—is a real compliment to Lady Alice's voice, and her rejection of its flattery the more poignant (as in the medieval romances and in Spenser, 'Courtesy' is an ethical, even religious virtue; not just being charming).

In paying his compliment, Comus distinguishes between her song and
the music of his world, the song of Circe and the Sirens:

> they in pleasing slumber lull'd the sense,
> And in sweet madnes rob'd it of it self,
> But such a sacred, and home-felt delight,
> Such sober certainty of waking bliss
> I never heard till now.

His music is jazz, lulling or frenzied, opiate or Dionysiac; it spellbinds,
drugs, ensnares; it makes the listener mad, beside himself. The Lady's
song reflects the rational, Olympian light that guides her; its god is
Apollo; and through a mythology popularised by Plato, and the im-
portance of music in his theories of the soul, ethics and education, it is
divine. For the Renaissance its divinity was practically Christian: for it
echoes the music made by the nine celestial spheres (parallel to the nine
orders of angels) as they revolve under the aegis of Apollo (identified
with Christ). This music only the innocent soul can hear:

> There's not the smallest orb which thou behold'st
> But in his motion like an angel sings,
> Still quiring to the young-eyed cherubins—
> Such harmony is in immortal souls;
> But whilst this muddy vesture of decay
> Doth grossly close it in, we cannot hear it.
> (*Merchant of Venice*, V. i. 50)

It symbolises the harmony—the original order and necessarily happy
ending—of the universe as created by God; it is

> the fair musick that all creatures made
> To their great Lord, whose love their motion sway'd
> In perfect Diapáson, whilst they stood
> In first obedience, and their state of good.
> (*At a Solemn Musick*)

It symbolises also the rational, stabilising power by which God created
the universe out of chaos—

> when of old the sons of morning sung,
> While the Creator Great
> His constellations set,
> And the well-balanc't world on hinges hung,

And cast the dark foundations deep,
And bid the weltring waves their oozy channel keep.
                              (*Nativity Ode*, 119)

It too enchants, but the spell releases the listener to a knowledge of the ordered good, 'Untwisting all the chains that ty The hidden soul of harmony' (*Il Penseroso*, 143). The physics of sound on which harmony is based form a natural (and, at that time, rarely empirical) symbol for harmony, in the body politic—

Take but degree away, untune that string,
And, hark, what discord follows!
                              (*Troilus & Cressida*, i. iii. 109)

—and, by analogy with heaven, in the soul, for music was therapeutic:

therefore the poet
Did feign that Opheus drew trees, stones, and floods;
Since naught so stockish, hard, and full of rage,
But music for the time doth change his nature.
                              (*Merchant of Venice*, V. i. 126)

This was a favourite theme of Milton's, and it is important to *Comus* The Elder Brother compliments Lawes, alias the Spirit, alias Thyrsis,

whose artful strains have oft delaid
The huddling brook to hear his madrigal,
And sweeten'd every muskrose of the dale ... (494)

—the good musician is a kind of Orpheus, able to charm natural experience into rational harmony (the compliment itself acts in an Orphean way: 'huddling' gives us knowledge of the brook, crouched bubbling over its stones; and the conceit asserts human superiority to nature). The Spirit had made the point when disguising himself as Thyrsis—

Who with his soft Pipe and smooth-dittied Song,
Well knows to still the wilde winds when they roar,
And hush the waving Woods. ... (86)

The pattern of injunctions to 'Hark' is being fulfilled.

5. The Brothers

Allegory

The Brothers seem the least allegorical parts in *Comus*. The Lady could be painted as Chastity attended by Conscience and leered at by Lust, with the Platonic form of Chastity, in the angelic shape of 'a glistering Guardian', gleaming through a cloud, and Virginity rising from a nearby fountain to protect her. In such favourite paintings of the Renaissance the Brothers would seem to us out of place. But Renaissance readers moved facilely between actual and abstract, particular and general. In this they were old wives—they had a penchant for proverbs. Their allegorical habit affected their attitude to language: they bodied forth what to us are mere figures of speech—'She's the soul of honesty' was not just a cliché. To us, allegorical characters are as unreal and hyperbolic as the figure of speech; for readers then, they referred to a super-real world in which the very archetype of Honesty did actually though invisibly exist. So the Brothers do have an allegorical tinge in the poem. They represent the male virtues of brotherliness, rationality (their debate) and courage—not only in their attack on Comus and their bravado in preparing for it but their reception of Thyrsis: 'What are you? speak; Com not too near, you fall on iron stakes else' (490) is in the heroic idiom of Elizabethan tragedy. Indeed, the characters represent all three elements in the Platonic constitution of the soul: Comus is the appetitive element, impulsively desiring physical goods; the Brothers, in their active role, are the 'spirited' element, impulsively desiring the immaterial good of honour; in their intellectual role they are the discursive faculty of the rational element; the Lady is intuitive reason.

Philosophy

The debate is a compliment to their education. It is similar to the debates in Latin prose in the Cambridge curriculum that Milton took part in. He preserved several he had written for these academic exercises. One is on the topic, 'Whether Day or Night is the more excellent', another 'On the Harmony of the Spheres'. Like the undergraduate Milton, the Brothers show off their learning by arguing in terms of classical authority, both philosophical ('shall I call Antiquity from the old

Schools of Greece . . . ?' [438]) and mythological ('Hence had the hun-
tress *Dian* her dred bow'). Between the end of Aristotle's medieval
reign and the beginning of modern epistemology in the seventeenth
century the distinction between philosophy and mythology was blurred,
as it is in Plato. So the Brothers' debate is at once a refutation of Comus's
jazz, magic and arguments, and a parallel to the Lady's harmony, grace
and instinctive immaculacy:

> How charming is divine Philosophy!
> Not harsh, and crabbèd as dull fools suppose,
> But musical as is *Apollo's* lute . . . (476)

Platonism

Both call for light, which stands for them and the Lady as the heaven-
sent token of reason and order in the world and in the soul. Then the
Elder Brother comforts the Younger by suggesting that the Lady, totally
rational, 'Wisdoms self', may have sought

> sweet retirèd Solitude,
> Where with her best nurse Contemplatiön
> She plumes her feathers, and lets grow her wings
> That in the various bussle of resort
> Were all to ruffl'd and somtimes impair'd. (376)

This use of Plato's bird simile for the soul is like stanzas vi–vii of Marvell's
Garden. The Elder Brother goes on:

> He that has light within his own cleer brest
> May sit i'th center, and enjoy bright day,
> But he that hides a dark soul, and foul thoughts
> Benighted walks under the mid-day Sun;
> Himself is his own dungeon.

This favourite theme of Milton's was to add horror to Samson's condition. It is based on Plato's assertion that the soul is superior to, and
transcends, the body; and only reason in the soul can apprehend the
genuine reality of the world of 'forms' where dwell absolute Honesty,
Chastity, Truth, Justice and so on; in the ordinary world only imitations
or shadows of these forms are available to our bodily senses. Although
all men have reason, only a few are so constituted as to desire, and apprehend, forms. These are the philosophers, lovers of wisdom. The Lady is
one—she has already seen the form of Chastity 'visibly' (215–16). This

theory of the soul and of the world of forms fitted in easily with Christian notions of the degradation of the body, and heaven; and the belief that only a few people were philosophers fitted the Christian—at any rate Calvinistic—belief that only a few were 'elect' to genuine faith and knowledge of God (and with the fact that only a few people are mystic).

The Younger Brother objects that, even so,

> beauty, like the fair Hesperian Tree
> Laden with blooming gold, had need the guard
> Of dragon watch with uninchanted eye,
> To save her blossoms, and defend her fruit
> From the rash hand of bold Incontinence. (393)

This is more in the ordinary pastoral tradition, where age-old metaphors and myths of beauty fused with the agricultural metaphors of sex, as in the *Faithful Shepherdess*:

> See, mine arms are full
> Of entertainment, ready for to pull
> That golden fruit which too, too long hath hung
> Tempting the greedy eye . . .

It also suggests what Yeats's 'dragon' means in *Michael Robartes and the Dancer* and *Her Triumph*.

Chastity

The Elder Brother answers first with simple optimism; his main answer, though, is divided between the doctrine of chastity, and a return to the doctrine of the soul. His ideas about the power of chastity are drawn from early fathers of the Church (such as St. Ambrose, bishop of Milan in the fourth century, author of a treatise *De Virginitate*) and from classical mythology. A rationalised mystique of virginity will be the product of individual psychology (Milton's personal phase at this time was one of sexual idealism), and of historical circumstance (Paul and Ambrose were struggling against pagan religions whose sexual cults and condonations devalued spirituality). Behind these lies a primitive taboo on virginity. Freud has discussed the rationale of this taboo; no doubt it includes, on the part of the man, fear of shedding blood by rupture of the hymen (symbolic murder), fear of being drowned or castrated by the woman, fear of losing power by sexual indulgence (a superstition Donne refers to in *Farewell to Love*).

The Elder Brother confuses chastity, which is an emotional condition, with virginity, which is a physical one with magical connotations. The case is confused further by the tendency to identify both with temperance.   According to Aristotle, temperance is the mean between two extremes: sexual temperance or emotional chastity would be the mean between two manifestations of impotence—obsessional celibacy, obsessional promiscuity. On this scale, Minerva's 'rigid looks of Chast austerity' (450), imputed to the Lady, would be intemperate. The confusion is due to mixing Aristotle's commonsensical psychological ethics with the idealist ethics and mythical psychology of Plato, and with accidental Christian elaborations on Paul's mysogyny.

The Soul

The Elder Brother strengthens his position when he returns to Plato. He says 'cleer dream, and solemn vision' tell the Lady 'of things that no gross ear can hear' (457)—that is, things of the Platonic world of forms, and of the Christian heaven, intimated by mystic vision and heaven-sent dream:

> Till oft convers with heav'nly habitants
> Begin to cast a beam on th'outward shape,
> The unpolluted temple of the mind,
> And turns it by degrees to the souls essence,
> Till all be made immortal. . . .

This is a conflation of Paul ('ye are the temple of God, and . . . the Spirit of God dwelleth in you' [1 Cor. iii. 16]) with Plato. Renaissance Platonists, elaborating on the *Symposium*, *Phaedrus* and *Phaedo*, held that the soul could work itself up by stages of contemplation from the love of individual physical objects (such as the beauty of women as observed by the senses) to knowledge of absolute immaterial Beauty, Love and so on, and ultimately to absorption into the godhead (as in Book IV of Castiglione's *Courtier* and in Spenser's Hymns to Heavenly Love and Beauty). The refinement of the soul resulting from this would affect the body. The Lady is safe from Comus's assaults, which are physical, because she is practically all soul, like Elizabeth Druty in Donne's *Funerall Elegie*:

> One, whose cleare body was so pure and thinne,
> Because it need disguise no thought within.
> 'Twas but a through-light scarfe, her mind t'inroule;
> Or exhalation breath'd out from her Soule. (59)

6. Thyrsis

Disguise

We have already referred to several passages in Thyrsis' encounter with the Brothers. Two points remain.

Firstly, the disguises common in masque come from the original masked dances. The good Spirit's disguise counters Comus's: on the one hand we have an allegory of the Good Shepherd (and all that's good in the natural pastoral life); on the other the false shepherd, the hireling—possibly with reformation hints of the *Lycidas* kind, certainly with indications of what is bad in pastoral.

Magic

Secondly, Thyrsis makes it clear that spiritual warfare needs spiritual weapons:

> Alas good ventrous youth,
> I love thy courage yet, and bold Emprise,
> But here thy sword can do thee little stead,
> Farr other arms, and other weapons must
> Be those that quell the might of hellish charms ... (609)

He produces haemony, a herb like the moly given by Hermes to Odysseus to guard him against Circe (*Odyssey*, X). Milton made up the name of his herb from Haemonia, which is Thessaly, the land of magic, guarded on one side by Olympus, the home of the gods. Herbs were actually medicinal, and conventionally redemptive, especially in pastoral; their roots were regarded as particularly 'virtuous' or therapeutic. Allegorically haemony stands for the virtue of temperance; dramatically, it is the talisman of white magic.

7. *Comus and the Lady*

Ethic and Aesthetic

Dramatically, Comus has no case: he has, as the Lady says, 'betray'd my credulous innocence with visor'd falsehood and base forgery', and now tries violence veneered as seductive logic. He does seem, though, to have a poetic case:

> When the fresh blood grows lively, and returns
> Brisk as the *April* buds in Primrose-season. (670)

>   millions of spinning Worms,
> That in their green shops weave the smooth-hair'd silk
> To deck her Sons . . . (715)

His language is empathetically involved in the things it refers to—it seems to enter into their being; whereas the Lady's language is abstract. You may judge Comus's poetry to be altogether better than the Lady's, especially if you think the world needs more sensitively inward apprehensions of actuality, and fewer layings-down of abstract and partially rational law. You might then say that these considerations prove Comus's case: in a poem, poetic practice is more potent than intellectual theory. So the masque cracks: the villain is hero, the heroine (as he says) cruel to herself, 'an ill borrower', unrealistically 'Scorning the unexempt condition By which all mortal frailty must subsist, Refreshment after toil, ease after pain' (685).

In the last resort it would be better to live by the acute sensibility that Comus's language implies (not the same as living by his ethic, of course), than by the defensive priggery implied by the Lady's language (which isn't, either, the same as her meaning). But we are not at the last resort. The primrose-season pleasures that Comus claims as peculiar to his palace are—as the scene shows—artificial and unreal. Instead of being the result of experience, of a real spring, of love, they are the fantasies 'That fancy can beget on youthfull thoughts' (669). Then his argument that the Lady is one of 'Those that have power to hurt and yet do none' (Shakespeare, Sonnet xciv) is exaggerated: she is not a professional virgin, not even an Emma Woodhouse, an Olivia. Thirdly, his speech is vitiated by its persuasiveness: 'none But such as are good men can give good things (702)'.

The Use of Nature

Comus's second speech is tricky. The Lady is not a Stoic or a Cynic. It begs the question to say that Nature poured her bounties forth 'to please and sate the curious taste'. The silkworms and the enwombed gems show the relation between commercial greed and sexual lust—Comus offers nature as a woman's body to be exploited, consumed: 'The expense of spirit in a waste of shame.' His next point rises to a threatening hyperbole of super-abundance which has no relation to its premiss. As his last point (739–57, omitted in the Ludlow production) Comus uses the *Vivamus, mea Lesbia* argument of Daniel's sonnet, 'When men shall find thy flower, thy glory, pass', and Marvell's *Coy Mistress*:

> If you let slip time, like a neglected rose
> It withers on the stalk with languish't head.

This is a stronger argument than it seems when you still have plenty of youth ahead of you; but again it is a case of exploitation—spending time and beauty for fear of losing them, instead of for love of someone else.

At Ludlow the Lady's reply was confined to lines 756–779a (followed by 806b). Comus's speech is so exciting that the Lady's rational case is often overlooked. But she makes a still-interesting link between temperance and democracy:

> If every just man that now pines with want
> Had but a moderate and beseeming share
> Of that which lewdly-pamper'd Luxury
> Now heaps upon som few with vast excess,
> Natures full blessings would be well dispenc't
> In unsuperfluous eeven proportion,
> And she no whit encomber'd with her store,
> And then the giver would be better thank't,
> His praise due paid, for swinish gluttony
> Ne're looks to Heaven amidst his gorgeous feast,
> But with besotted base ingratitude
> Cramms, and blasphemes his feeder. (768)

This is true—politically, of the gap between our affluent society and the starvation of Asia; and individually, of the 'consumer' of 'goods'. It isn't that he's wrong to have a three-piece suite, but that he consumes it wrongly, and wrongly regards it as a good. The suite may be a substitute for, and displace, some richer good (peace, joy). His purchase may even be merely a case of 'conspicuous consumption', a symbol of his income-bracket (or his credit), and not a thing to sit on at all.

Intuition

The lady's second argument does not appeal to discursive reason, but intuition, or conscience. She does not sufficiently realise in poetry 'The sublime notion, and high mystery' of virginity to justify Comus's fearful reaction (800); but we have seen enough of the theories of harmony and the soul to realise what is intended here without our being guilty of the 'intentional fallacy': the intention is apparent in the masque as a whole, and the sources of its sentiments. This is the final argument against Comus: if we feel he (for all his motives) is possessed of an intuition about the world that is valuable, here we have the Lady (for all the possible falsities of her chastity) also expressing an intuition, a claim to spiritual apprehension. It is no longer a case of passion against reason, nature against law; black magic is met with white, spirit by spirit. Of course the debate is irresoluble: the Lady shuts her ears to Comus's music, believing that her apprehension of the truth is superior; while Comus has 'not Eare, nor Soul to apprehend' her ideal.

8. Sabrina

Sabrina is the goddess of the local river, the Severn. Rivers were then important as means of communication and defence (and, in this case, the boundary between England and Wales); so the episode introduces the Bridgewaters to the geography of their new home, propitiates the local deities and acknowledges their cults—

> For which the Shepherds at their festivals
> Carrol her goodnes lowd in rustick layes,
> And throw sweet garland wreaths into her stream
> Of pancies, pinks, and gaudy Daffadils. (848)

Milton took the story of Sabrina from the *Faerie Queene* (II. x. 14–19).
Spenser was the most popular English poet of the time and Milton's
acknowledgment—

> Which once of *Meliboeus* old I learnt
> The soothest Shepherd that ere pip't on plains (822)

—reaches out of the masque into the literary world that the Derby and
Bridgewater families were so closely connected with.

The Spirit's farewell blessing on Sabrina is thus a prayer for the dis-
trict's prosperity. Then, master of the revels, he hurries his charges back
into the plot towards the culminating ceremony. All this makes an hospitable setting for the anti-masque of local country-dancers. They are
dismissed—'Back, shepherds back; enough your play' (958)—to make
way for the central courtly dance. Then the children are presented to
the Earl and Countess, and the occasion is complete.

9. *Epilogue*

In the acting version the epilogue consisted only of the last twelve
lines. We must consider it as it stands in the literary version, because it
is an attempt to synthesise the thesis and antithesis of the action. The
last 'Hark!'—'List mortals, if your ears be true'—introduces a world
like the bower of Venus and Adonis in the *Faerie Queene*, III. vi. 43–50.
In Milton's elysium

> young *Adonis* oft reposes,
> Waxing well of his deep wound
> In slumber soft, and on the ground
> Sadly sits th'*Assyrian* Queen . . . (999)

Venus ('th'Assyrian Queen') is the goddess of natural love; she can never
be satisfied because her mate, Adonis, is the god of natural life which
must annually suffer winter's wound. Spenser suggests that the annual
resurrection of life transcends death—'eterne in mutability'. Milton
here offers something else:

> But farr above in spangled sheen
> Celestial *Cupid* her fam'd son, advanc't,
> Holds his dear *Psyche* sweet intranc't

> After her wandring labours long,
> Till free consent the gods among
> Make her his eternal Bride,
> And from her fair unspotted side
> Two blissful twins are to be born,
> Youth and Joy; so *Jove* hath sworn.

The story of Cupid and Psyche (told in Apuleius's *Golden Ass*) was popular in the Renaissance because it could be read partly as an allegory on the Platonic and Christian union of the soul with the form of Love and the love of God; the issue is time-defying youth and joy. Milton adds it to the gardens of the sun where the Hesperides and their dragon (cf. line 393) guard the apples of love; this is the Spirit's abode. Together, these allusions imply that the Spirit's aid is not magisterial, nor the Lady's chastity chilly. Youthful chastity, with its passion for ideal beauty, is promised a consummation which is spiritual but also intensely delightful, and productive, and so more real than Comus's selfish sensuality—'loveless, joyless, unindeard, Casual fruition' (*P.L.* IV. 766). The epilogue is confusing, and may be suspected of trying to have it both ways; yet we recognise something like its voluptuous innocence briefly in our own experience of genuine love.

10. *The Verse*

Because it has to serve the several forms contained in masque, the verse of *Comus* exhibits extraordinary variety. There is colloquial idiom such as 'The leaf was darkish, and had prickles on it' (631), belonging to the real shepherds of pastoral, though bits of it toughen all the speeches, even in mythological contexts—'This dim spot, Which men call Earth'. There is extravagant naturalistic metaphor and personification of the Elizabethan kind: 'th'unsought diamonds Would so emblaze the forehead of the Deep' (732); this is mostly Comus's, of course. But only one side of the Renaissance mind was sensuous and materialistic, and even that—as here—tended to flare off into aspirations so impossible as to be abstract. Its other side was solemnly idealistic, but correspondingly checked by a sense of the concrete: 'The soul grows clotted by contagion'

(467). But the verse as a whole does not reconcile these varieties or commit itself to any one of them. It wings from one to the other, displaying its own astonishing virtuosity. The variations in tone and tempo are remarkable, and sometimes, as in the Elder Brother's speech starting at line 418, locally significant; but the Spirit's at 513 moves with merely delightful skill between the extremes of Ovidian conceit—

> the drowsie frighted steeds
> That draw the litter of close-curtain'd sleep

—and Juliet's-Nurse-like talk:

> And, 'O poor hapless nightingale,' thought I.

Historically, the verse exhibits just what one would expect: nostalgic mitation, at a clarifying distance, of various Elizabethan kinds such as Spenserian smoothness, and the prettier passages of Shakespearean comedy (though with some glances at melodrama: 'Unmuffle ye faint stars' [331]); a drift into the hollower sensuousness of *rococo* ('the rosie-bosom'd Howres'); and a strong move towards the abstract vocabulary, heavy stresses and intellectual syntax of Milton's later poems and the eighteenth century:

> Vertue may be assail'd, but never hurt,
> Surpriz'd by unjust force, but not enthrall'd ... (589)

The action and ideology of the masque suggest, rather than realise, ideals of harmony, fruition and so on; in the same way the verse lacks an assured norm that would draw and shape its virtuosity into a recognisably individual act. It is like one dancing in delight over the earth, then sometimes falling to more solemn tread, sometimes taking flight to another world:

> I can fly, or I can run
> Quickly to the green earths end,
> Where the bow'd welkin slow doth bend,
> And from thence can soar as soon
> To the corners of the Moon.

It is a case of sheer mimetic power—the basic genius of poetry—operating with quite simple materials, of course, and expressing conventional sentiments; but keeping itself wonderfully alive, unanxious and free within the strict decorum of the genre. It is a supreme example of courtesy as the Renaissance saw it—not just manners, 'style', but a way of living in which spontaneity acts harmoniously within convenient rules, as Yeats sees the dancer and the dance unified at the end of his poem *Among Schoolchildren*. Yeats, though he thought quite differently from Milton about passion, prayed for his daughter, 'In courtesy I'd have her chiefly learned', for

> How but in custom and in ceremony
> Are innocence and beauty born?

SAMSON AGONISTES

1. *Introduction*

Samson and Tragedy

If we were now to write something about Samson it would probably be a short poem shuffling the mythological, psychological and symbolic materials latent in the legend, rather in the manner of Roy Fuller or Edwin Muir. A good deal of such material was available to Milton, from his knowledge of Hebrew and of ancient culture generally; from his familiarity with the many commentaries on *Judges*; and from the traditional interpretation of Biblical stories. Interpretation was threefold: moral or tropological—courage is good, betraying secrets bad; allegorical or typological—Samson, who is mighty and whose name means 'sun', is a type of Christ the sun of righteousness and son of God; and symbolic or anagogic—Samson represents the contemplative mind illumined by divine knowledge, cast into the dark night of the soul, then retrieved, and so on. The moral and allegorical interpretations were presented in the popular devotional literature of the seventeenth century—sermons, emblem-books (illustrated object-lessons) and such things as the *History of Samson* published in 1631 by Francis Quarles: a turgid versification of all the episodes in Samson's life with sermonisings in between. The Metaphysical poets often used typology: in his poem 'Sunday', Herbert related Samson's carrying away of the gates of Gaza to Christ's resurrection:

> The rest of our Creation
> Our great Redeemer did remove
> With the same shake, which at his passion
> Did th'earth and all things with it move.
> As Samson bore the doores away,
> Christs hands, though nail'd, wrought our salvation,
> And did unhinge that day.

But Milton extends the myth beyond a Metaphysical metaphor, and treats it in a distinctly unpopular medium. Classically modelled tragedy had never been popular: Jonson, whose 'learned Sock' even Milton admired, excused himself for not obeying the Aristotelian rules and not having a proper chorus in his *Sejanus* (1603) by saying:

Nor is it needful, or almost possible in these our times, and to such auditors as commonly things are presented, to observe the old state and splendor of dramatic poems with preservation of any popular delight.

Milton in his preface claims to 'vindicate tragedy from the small esteem, or rather infamy, which in the account of many it undergoes at this day with other common Interludes'. His account of the tragic effect is only a rehash of Aristotle's homeopathic purge theory; but it accords with his own therapeutic and didactic, yet celebratory theory of art. Poetic genius, he said in one of his pamphlets, is 'the inspired gift of God', able, as well as preaching, to

imbreed and cherish in a great people the seeds of virtue and public civility, to allay the perturbations of the mind, and set the affections in right tune ... to sing victorious agonies of martyrs and saints, the deeds and triumphs of just and pious nations, doing valiantly through faith against the enemies of Christ ... (*Reason of Church Government*; Bohn, ii. 479).

So he pleads for public theatres to work with the pulpit against vice. The theatres were closed next year, so *Samson* was not for the stage.

It is, then, like many of Milton's poems, a theoretical or ideal work, displaying what might be done with the form rather than what could be done with real live actors, audience, readers. He was not deluded: in every age there are writers fiercely concerned to replace the popular tosh by a literature they believe will have better ethical and political effect. In Milton's own time many other writers (such as Jonson) had tried to classicise the drama, and to christianise it, or both (e.g. George Buchanan, who wrote Latin plays about Jephtha and John the Baptist in the sixteenth century, and the Dutch poet Vondel, who wrote a *Samson* in 1660). But it never works. Milton, anxious to purify tragedy with classicism, and christen it with a Biblical story, tested form and content almost to destruction. *Samson Agonistes* is actually more regularly Aristotelian in construction than any extant Greek tragedy (so it is a misleading introduction to the plays of Aeschylus, Sophocles and Euripides). Extreme regularity of form is matched by extreme finality of plot. Since the later Middle Ages, devotional and literary works about Samson had shifted interest from the earlier episodes of mere violence in Samson's life to the more psychological episodes involving Delilah; but the last episode had never been popular with writers or painters. In concentrating on the catastrophe Milton went beyond both popularity and Greek tragedy. The action of a Greek trilogy, based on myths covering several generations, was cyclic rather than final, ending as often as not in compromise: Oedipus does not die, he is at first exiled, then translated, and his daughters continue the plot. But *Samson* is final; and its finality deprives it of movement in place or time, and of any kind of discovered secret, dropped handkerchief, oracle or apparition, such as complicate and naturalise Sophocles' plays, and even Aeschylus' static *Prometheus Bound*.

Style

The style also is extreme; but here, instead of commitment to extreme classical authority, we have the expression of eccentric personal talent. The verse could not, in the seventeenth century, nearer approach what was then prose, yet still so assertively be verse as this:

> *Off.* Rise therefore with all speed and come along, where I will see thee
> heartened and fresh clad to appear as fits before the illustrious lords.
> *Sam.* Thou know'st I am an Ebrew: therefore tell them our law for-
> bids at their religious rites my presence: for that cause, I cannot
> come.
> *Off.* This answer, be assured, will not content them.
> *Sam.* Have they not sword-players and every sort of gymnic artists,
> wrestlers, riders, runners, jugglers and dancers, antics, mummers,
> mimics, but they must pick me out, with shackles tired and over-
> laboured at their public mill, to make them sport with blind activity?
> Do they not seek occasion of new quarrels, on my refusal to distress
> me more, or make a game of my calamities? Return the way thou
> cam'st, I will not come.
> *Off.* Regard thyself, this will offend them highly.
> *Sam.* My self? My conscience and internal peace! (1317)

In the last three lines speech-rhythms emphasise meaning against the metrical pattern: 'Re*turn* the *way* thou *cam'st*: *I will not come*'; 'My *self*? My *con*science and in*ter*nal peace!' These tensions symbolise or complement the strain that Samson's roused individuality is now putting on his captivity—the strain the Messenger will directly mime:

> those two massie Pillars
> With horrible convulsion to and fro,
> He tugg'd, he shook, till down they came and drew
> The whole roof after them . . . (1648)

But, apart from the context, the words are all along clashing against the metre, yet being contained tightly within it. Even when the lines go supple and idiomatic, a phrase will jut out to remind one that it all is art: 'To make them sport with *blind activity*'. Again, at the end of the triumphant semichorus:

> So fond are mortal men
> Fall'n into wrath divine,
> As thir own ruin on themselves to invite,
> Insensate left, or to sense reprobate,
> And with blindness internal struck. (1682)

The verse and sense clang and muddle in the penultimate line, then clarify ferociously into 'And with blindness internal struck', taken up and rhymed-into by the next semichorus to assert the nature of Samson's victory:

> But he though blind of sight,
> Despis'd and though extinguish't quite,
> With inward eyes illuminated . . .

The actual sentiments are not often complicated; but the expression of them is packed, jostling and contorted, sometimes—as in Samson's 'O dark, dark, dark'—almost surrealistic.

It is especially the rhythm of the odes, though, that had been unheard ever before in English: they display a technical originality unequalled until Hopkins. These four lines alone are more subtly incantatory than anything before 'Tiger, tiger, burning bright':

> *Oh* how *comely* it is // and how re*viv*ing
> To the *Spirits* of *just men long* opp*rest*!//
> When *God* into the *hands* of thir de*liv*erer
> *Puts* // in*vin*cible *might* . . .

Now this unheard-of, unprecedented verse clashes against the ancient authority of the form; their clash echoes the collision of the terrible Old Testament myth with Christian doctrine. These collisions are characteristic of Milton's work: highly individuated talent striving to realise itself but anxious all the time to be authorised by tradition—a filial talent excusing itself to paternal authority.

Talent

Talent is the crux for Samson: Why did God give me strength of
body, and send an angel to prophesy my birth, if I was to fail?

Milton himself was conscious of highest worth; but he spent many
years as a young man being kept by his father; he could not settle to a
job. When the revolution started in 1640 he seized on it as an arena for
his talents, but it eventually collapsed. At the beginning of it he made a
mistaken marriage; in the middle of it he went blind:

> When I consider how my light is spent,
>   E're half my days, in this dark world and wide,
>   And that one Talent which is death to hide,
>   Lodg'd with me useless, though my Soul more bent
> To serve therewith my Maker, and present
>   My true account, least he returning chide,
>   Doth God exact day-labour, light deny'd,
>   I fondly ask . . .

Milton used Samson more publicly in his prose sometimes, but his
major allusions are allegories written with a personal intensity. In *The
Reason of Church Government* (1641) he likened a king to

> that mighty Nazarite . . . who being disciplined from his birth in the
> precepts and the practice of temperance and sobriety, without the
> strong drink of injurious and excessive desires, grows up to a noble
> strength and perfection with those his illustrious and sunny locks, the
> laws, waving and curling about his godlike shoulders. And while he
> keeps them about him undiminished and unshorn, he may with the
> jawbone of an ass, that is, with the word of his meanest officer, sup-
> press and put to confusion thousands of those that rise against his just
> power. But laying down his head among the strumpet flatteries of
> prelates, while he sleeps and thinks no harm, they wickedly shaving
> off all those bright and weighty tresses of his law, and just prerogatives ,
> which were his ornament and strength, deliver him over to indirect
> and violent counsels, which, as those Philistines, put out the fair and
> far-sighted eyes of his natural discerning, and make him grind in the
> prisonhouse of their sinister ends and practices upon him: till he,
> knowing this prelatical rasor to have bereft him of his wonted might,
> nourish again his puissant hair, the golden beams of law and right; and
> they sternly shook, thunder with ruin upon the heads of those his evil
> counsellors, but not without great affliction to himself.   (ii. 506)

The apocalyptic conclusion is similar to Milton's vision in *Areopagitica*:

> Methinks I see in my mind a noble and puissant nation [England]
> rousing herself like a strong man after sleep, and shaking her invincible
> locks: methinks I see her as an eagle mewing her mighty youth, and
> kindling her undazzled eyes at the full midday beam; purging and un-
> scaling her long-abused sight at the fountain itself of heavenly radiance;
> while the whole noise of timorous and flocking birds, with those that
> flutter about, amazed at what she means . . .
>
> (ii. 94)

In the *Doctrine and Discipline of Divorce* Samson is not the symbol of re-
generated political power but he is, implicitly, the symbol of love. Eros
finds he is ill-matched—

> and that original and fiery virtue given him by fate all an a sudden
> goes out, and leaves him undeified and dispoiled of all his force . . .

This is part of Milton's protest against being forced 'to grind in the mill
of an undelighted and servile copulation' (iii. 196). But when Eros finds
his true mate, Anteros, at last,

> he kindles and repairs the almost-faded ammunition of his deity by the
> reflection of a coequal and homogeneal fire.

Samson's mill is partly 'the dark Satanic mills' of Blake—the punitive
repression of genius in all its forms.

2. Commentary

Note. I use the divisions of a tragedy as Aristotle gives them in his
Poetics.

Prologos (1–114)

> My words echo thus in your memory
>
> (T. S. Eliot.)

When Milton's words echo in your memory it isn't usually as it is with
Shakespeare that they've made things new by breeding the familiar—
'procreant cradle'; but that, plain, indicative, moodily cerebral, they

define and establish what is already well known, and then fix it in the
poem and in Milton's theodicy:

> A little onward lend they guiding hand
> To these dark steps, a little further on;

These words won't echo in your mind unless you're conscious of having
needed desperately the hand of lover or parent. But they do echo in the
poem. It is the hand of one who leads Samson on to the stage, and the
familiarity with the Bible story expected by Milton identifies it with
God's hand, and with 'the lad that led him by the hand' between the
pillars at the end. That is the 'little onward' that he has to go: it is the
distance between darkness and illumination:

> Judge me, O God, and plead my cause against the ungodly nation:
> O deliver me from the deceitful and unjust man. For thou art the God
> of my strength; why dost thou cast me off? Why go I in mourning
> because of the oppression of the enemy? O send out thy light and thy
> truth: let them lead me . . .
>
> (*Ps.* xliii)

Before Samson can find God at the feast of Dagon he has to be re-
newed in faith. At first, he enjoys a merely physical revival:

> but here I feel amends,
> The breath of Heav'n fresh-blowing, pure and sweet,
> With day-spring born . . .

But for the audience these words indicate the trend of the plot for they
echo the *Benedictus*:

> the day-spring from on high hath visited us, to give light to them that
> sit in darkness and in the shadow of death, to guide our feet into the
> way of peace.
>
> (*Lk.* i. 78)

That is from Zacharias' prophecy at the birth of his son John the Baptist.
Like Samson, John's birth was foretold by an angel and his death in-
stigated by a woman, Salome.

The contrast between this fresh air and the prison's unwholesome
draught is the first of a series of contrasts in Samson's prologue. Next is
one between 'the popular noise' and 'This unfrequented place', this
solitary bank. In *Comus* the Spirit says he had

> sate me down to watch upon a bank
> With Ivy canopied, and interwove
> With flaunting Hony-suckle, and began
> Wrapt in a pleasing fit of melancholy
> To meditate my rural minstrelsie,
> Till fancy had her fill . . .
>
> (543)

Samson's meditations are to be more stringent; but, like the Spirit's, they are interrupted by 'barbarous dissonance'. Samson has got to die amidst 'the popular noise' he has now retired from. For Milton that always meant chaos. It was philistine in Matthew Arnold's sense, for it destroyed the harmony of art and of the temperate life; it was also an image of the destruction of the artist himself by the female agency of the bacchantes,

> that wilde Rout that tore the *Thracian* Bard
> In *Rhodopë*, where Woods and Rocks had Eares
> To rapture, till the savage clamor dround
> Both Harp and Voice;
>
> (*P.L.* VII. 32; *cf. Lycidas*)

Samson is to redeem himself and the temperate culture he is the champion of, not, as the artist usually does, by withdrawing from the philistines, but by going to meet them. But before he is fit to meet that public hostility he has to cope with the stinging swarm of his own 'restless thoughts'. The heroic future can be reached only by reconciling a third contrast, between 'what once I was, and what am now'.

Samson with chagrin wonders why he was attended with so much grace—the angel of his birth, his breeding as a Nazarite, his strength: the burden of talents. He sees the failure of this grace as his own fault, but sees it in a drily objective way:

> Promise was that I
> Should *Israel* from *Philistian* yoke deliver;
> Ask for this great Deliverer now, and find him
> Eyeless in *Gaza* at the Mill with slaves,
> Himself in bonds under Philistian yoke;

The line-ending stresses on 'I' and 'him' here are a little sign that he hasn't yet fully identified his innermost self with the failed Samson he is contemplating. The same thin objectivity marks his acknowledgments of God's will as half-hearted because divided in heart:

> Yet stay, let me not rashly call in doubt
> Divine Prediction;
>
> But peace, I must not quarrel with the will
> Of highest dispensation,

So far, he admits but does not realise his own fault. He does realise
though the weakness of his strength:

> God, when he gave me strength, to shew withal
> How slight the gift was, hung it in my Hair.

The lightness of the last clause shows him tossing the gift aside almost.
What he has to do later in the action is accept the talent of strength in all
its burdensomeness and with all its frailties.

Now, having at a human level abandoned pride in his strength, he
turns to the worst of his present evils, loss of sight. This ode shows signs
of having been put together from at least two pieces written at different
times, so it is difficult to read coherently. Its text is from the New Testament lesson for 13 April, when the other lesson is *Judges* xv, about
Samson:

> The light of the body is the eye: therefore when thine eye is single,
> thy whole body also is full of light; but when thine eye is evil, thy
> body also is full of darkness. Take heed therefore that the light that is
> in thee be not darkness. (*Lk*. xi. 34)

The exile which Samson is mainly concerned with here is from the
natural world 'and all her various objects of delight' which assure him
of God's creating hand; and from the world of men (as Milton put it in
his sonnet *To Mr. Cyriack Skinner, on his Blindness*, and in the invocation
at *Paradise Lost* III). His blindness is Samson's excuse for lack of faith.
From the echoing eloquence of 'O dark, dark, dark', where his mouth
seems turned to the sky, the lyric lowers and narrows under the pressure
of environing darkness (the argument 'why was the sight To such a
tender ball as th' eye confin'd' conveys the sufferer's sense of con-
centrated pain) until his whole being is absorbed in the vulnerability and
extinction of sight. This structural movement is paralleled in the rhetorical details, where by a series of plays upon words Samson identifies
light with delight and life, and darkness with death. The hideous irony
is that, being dark-dead, he still appears, from outside, as light-alive: he is
protesting ultimately against the grind of having to live without vitality.

A theme that runs all through the poem is Samson's horror of exposure to mockery, 'still as a fool'. He thinks the approaching Chorus are enemies 'come to stare At my affliction, and perhaps to insult, Thir daily practice to afflict me more'.

Parode (115–175)

The Chorus come on Samson with a curious lulling rhythm—

>   This, this is he; softly a while,
>   Let us not break in upon him;

—and then see him, vaguely, as a storm-smashed flower. Against these they put a celebration of Samson's might; then they return to his present condition and present his blindness, as he had done, in terms of the self's imprisonment; finally, they define him as a tragic hero, in terms of heroic strength. Here Samson, so far revealed, though half objectively, in his own terms, as one reviled, is seen with real objectivity, from outside; first with pity for what he is now, then admiration for what he was. Samson has enacted his present impotence; the Chorus enact his past might—'Ran on embattelld Armies clad in Iron' (129)—with clattering boisterousness. Then, where Samson had seen himself as an object of scorn, the Chorus see him as an example of fortune's fickleness (165).

1st Episode: Samson and Chorus (176–292)

Samson's couplet with its mourning vowels—

>   I hear the sound of words, thir sense the air
>   Dissolves unjointed e're it reach my ear (176)

—stretches the distance between the subjective and objective views. When Samson goes back on his own ode and says it is not blindness but shame that grieves him most, it is not so much a development of his mood as an alteration in it to suit his now more public situation. The Chorus show the possibility of development within him by their reply—'Deject not then so overmuch thy self' (213). Though pious, this is merely sensible human comfort based on ordinary human weakness—'wisest Men Have err'd'. It denies heroism. Yet they anxiously assert him as a tragic hero of the conventional type, one who 'from the top of wondrous glory' is fallen 'To lowest pitch of abject fortune'. It is a crude theory of tragedy, and the possibility they see in Samson—

>   whose strength, while vertue was her mate,
>   Might have subdued the Earth,
>   Universally crown'd with highest praises (173)

—is cruder still, and false to the Biblical story. This is because the Chorus have to justify Samson externally as hero and martyr. Samson has to be excused especially for sexual irregularities. He had married a Philistine, the woman of Timnath (*Judges* xiv). Then (*Judges* xvi) he visited a prostitute in Gaza. Thirdly, he fell in love with Delilah. His feats of sex and strength are understandable to the anthropologist, who sees Samson as a local strong man credited with magical power, and, perhaps, a sun-god; but they had always worried the theologians. At the Renaissance especially, the spirit of rationalistic inquiry—the beginnings of independent Biblical criticism and of critical and comparative theology—combined with Puritan sentiment and a literal reading of the texts, exaggerated these awkwardnesses into serious problems, to be 'solved' by the kind of rationalising excuses that the Chorus indulge in here.

1st Stasimon (293-325)

Bound up with the problem of Samson's promiscuity is his claim of 'intimate impulse' (233) authorising his betrothal to the woman of Timnath as a means of advancing his country's cause. If, of course, he did marry her only to 'begin *Israel's* Deliverance', he was as guilty as he says Delilah was in allowing 'Private respects' to yield to 'Public good' (867). But this is to follow the poem's false trail: we must leave logic-chopping to Milton's Chorus, only observing two things. First, the question of prompting by some inner voice, of conscience, is left in abeyance so far as Samson's earlier acts are concerned:

> thou didst plead
> Divine impulsion prompting how thou might'st
> Find some occasion to infest our Foes.
> I state [argue] not that; this I am sure; our Foes
> Found soon occasion thereby to make thee
> Thir Captive, and thir triumph; thou the sooner
> Temptation found'st . . . (421)

says Manoah. But Samson's heroic end is to be the issue of conscience too: 'I begin to feel Some rouzing motions in me' (1381). In short, the virtue of 'conscience' must be judged by its issue, and perhaps also by the mood in which it is listened to; for Samson, it works when he is chastened, but brings disaster when he is cocksure. But the poem does no more than *Comus* to analyse that dangerous faculty. Indeed, the second

point to make is that the Chorus are wrong: they say men must trust
God, even when he seems to condone the breaking of his own laws by
conscience-driven men; and they conclude:

> Down Reason then, at least vain reasonings down,
> Though Reason here aver
> That moral verdict quits her [woman of Timnath] of unclean:
> Unchaste was subsequent, her stain, not his. (322)

As the little extra bit of logic-chopping shows, the motive for faith as
against reason is here itself rationalistic. The same thing happens when
the Chorus exculpate Samson from suicide (another anxiety of the commentators):

> self-kill'd
> Not willingly, but tangl'd in the fold
> Of dire necessity, whose law in death conjoin'd
> Thee with thy slaughter'd foes in number more
> Then all thy life had slain before. (1664)

The only necessity that can matter in the poem is that within Samson
himself, driving him to a public end; when it is stated philosophically it
is ineffectual, and the argument slides off into gruesome praise. These
passages prove Keats's dictum, 'Beauty is truth, truth beauty.' You
might think poetry would help a bad argument; it exposes it. So Samson's fine scorn—his first public activity in the play—about nations
which 'love Bondage more than Liberty' (270) is vitiated by its context of
self-justification; and the Chorus's traditional placing of him with
Gideon is spoilt by Samson's threatening growl—

> Mee easily mine may neglect,
> But Gods propos'd deliverance not so. (291)

The tragedy does not purge him of this God-invoking self-righteous-
ness: it was a characteristic of Milton's age which he was far from
transcending in himself.

2nd Episode: Samson and Manoah (326-651)

The episode with Manoah advances the action some way. He is a
'character', tempting with kindly weakness where the play's other
'character', Haraphah, will tempt with hostile strength. His first speech
(340-72) causes Samson to make in public the rebuke he has already made

to himself: 'Appoint not heavenly disposition, Father'. But in making it public his private understanding of the situation becomes more acute:

> Nothing of all these evils hath befall'n me
> But justly; I my self have brought them on,
> Sole Author I, sole cause:

He lifts himself a little way out of despair by recognising that

> The base degree to which I now am fall'n,
> These rags, this grinding, is not yet so base
> As was my former servitude, ignoble,
> Unmanly, ignominious, infamous,
> True slavery, and that blindness worse then this,
> That saw not how degenerately I serv'd. (414)

Looking back on his past with this much understanding, he is better able to deal accurately with the present. When Manoah tells him that the Philistines are going to sacrifice to Dagon in gratitude for capturing Samson, Samson withdraws *hors de combat*: 'all the contést is now 'Twixt God and *Dagon*' (461). But Manoah (whose name means 'rest') tempts him to withdraw further, into ransomed ease. Samson, speaking wearily— 'Spare that proposal, Father, spare the trouble Of that sollicitation' (487) —abandons himself rather to his punishment: his indiscretion has made him unfit for company (again the sense of being an object of contempt). Manoah's reply is psychologically sensible:

> Repent the sin, but if the punishment
> Thou canst avoid, self-preservation bids; (504)

To insist, whatever God's will, on punishment, would suggest being 'over-just, and self-displeas'd For self-offence, more then for God offended'. Samson now sees himself clear-eyed: what would be the use of living at home, 'To visitants a gaze', in 'a contemptible old age obscure'? When he had useful strength he abused it; better now to 'drudge and earn my bread' than 'to sit idle on the household hearth A burdenous drone'. This view of himself is more complete and dispassionate, yet more fully admitted, than his earlier ones; but the motif is still that of his first speech, 'still as a fool, In power of others, never in my own; Scarce half I seem to live, dead more then half' (77). Now, though, his brittle ode on living death is translated into a speech which is at once the most expressive in the play and the most viable for the reader's experience and imagination:

> So much I feel my genial spirits droop,
> My hopes all flat, nature within me seems
> In all her functions weary of herself;
> My race of glory run, and race of shame,
> And I shall shortly be with them that rest. (594)

Manoah interjects a few lines of fussy comfort; they are irrelevant to Samson because, though now at his nadir, he has attained by this speech a stature which the other characters cannot approach. The enacted collapse of Samson's bass drooping spirits speech isolates him from the ordinary run of men represented by Manoah's quick silly cheer. The quenched sensations of his first ode are replaced by an excruciating pain inextricably physical and mental at once—

> Thoughts my Tormenters arm'd with deadly stings
> Mangle my apprehensive tenderest parts. (623)

The images are unoriginal and repetitive without being helpfully consistent (the stings start at line 19 as 'a deadly swarm Of Hornets arm'd' but they are confused with exernal pains such as the 'Scorpions tail' in God's gifts [360] and the sting [997, 1001, 1007] and thorn [1037] of Delilah). There are moments in this ode when we semantically grasp something: 'mortification' in line 622, for instance, offers in its double sense of gangrene and chagrin something for us to hold on to; mostly though we hear tonal arrangements, such as the fluctuating lament of the first line, then word-by-word teeth-gritting emphasis, and sudden collapse, of

> Left me all helpless with th' irreparable loss
> Of sight, reserv'd alive to be repeated
> The subject of their cruelty, or scorn.
> Nor am I in the list of them that hope;
> Hopeless are all my evils, all remédiless; (644)

This constructs a pattern out of the *loss*, *-less*, and *re-* words; but it is only the tone of voice suggested by them, not the words themselves, that leads us into the experience.

2nd Stasimon (652–709)

The Chorus (667) paraphrase Job:

> What is man, that thou shouldest magnify him?
> And that thou shouldest visit him every morning, and try him every moment?

> How long wilt thou not depart from me, nor let me alone till I
>   swallow down my spittle?
> I have sinned; what shall I do unto thee, O thou preserver of men?
>   why has thou set me as a mark against thee, so that I am a burden to
>   myself?
> And why dost thou not pardon my transgression, and take away mine
>   iniquity? (vii. 17)

The ode has the peculiar confused muted air of dry-eyed prose assertion
exalted into a hymn of defiance on waves of fluctuant rhythm which
bounce against heaven and drop back again—'Amidst thir highth of
noon . . . condemnation of the ingrateful multitude'.

In the episode with Manoah, Samson and the Chorus had digressed on
the virtue of Nazarite temperance, celebrating 'the cool Crystalline
stream', 'the clear milkie [transparent] juice' (546). 'What avail'd this
temperance,' Samson had asked, 'not compleat Against another object
more enticing?' Into his ode Samson had let similar tastes of the healing
freshness desired in his first soliloquy—'breath of Vernal Air from snowy
Alp' (628); but they were ineffectual, he was left with 'deaths be-num-
ming Opium as my only cure'. The Chorus realise that only this kind
of salvation, 'Secret refreshings', can now 'repair his strength, And faint-
ing spirits uphold' (665); and at the end of their stasimon they plead for
Samson in liturgical rhythm: 'So deal not with this once thy glorious
Champion' (705). Then, realising they have accidentally prayed, they
become colloquial: 'What do I beg? how hast thou dealt already?' But
then revert to a neutrally toned request:

> Behold him in this state calamitous, and turn
> His labours, for thou canst, to peaceful end.

The effect of all these passages is to introduce, at Samson's nadir, the
possibility of a more than physical revival. The Chorus have no hope,
but a faint breath of faith; Samson, self-knowing now but still absorbed
in his self-knowledge, has neither faith nor hope. His 'sense of Heav'ns
desertion' (632) is the despair which is a Christian sin, but from it greater
faith may spring. So Hopkins cries:

> Not, I'll not, carrion comfort, Despair, not feast on thee;
> Not untwist—slack they may be—these last strands of man
> In me or, most weary, cry 'I can no more'. I can.

And for Eliot it is through the dark night of the soul that one must pass
to reach the light of God's will:

Internal darkness, deprivation
And destitution of all property,
Desiccation of the world of sense,
Evacuation of the world of fancy,
Inoperancy of the world of spirit;
This is the one way, and the other
Is the same, not in movement
But abstention from movement; while the world moves
In appetency, on its metalled ways
Of time past and time future.

(*Burnt Norton*)

3rd Episode: Samson and Delilah (710–1009)

Now on the rails of appetency Delilah appears, ironically like one of those refreshing gusts, 'Sails fill'd, and streamers waving, Courted by all the winds that hold them play' (718). She tempts Samson with various comforts: flattery—her desire to see him, her love as the excuse for having him caught; the comforting companionship of sin—'Let weakness then with weakness come to parl' (785); the comforts of marriage. In rejecting these temptations Samson admits publicly, to his worst enemy, all his weakness. In addition, he moves out of the slough of despond into intelligent action and puts himself firmly beyond ordinary mortality. Thus when he refuses the truce of mutual weakness, because 'All wickedness is weakness' (834), he refuses a relativism which would have made nonsense not only of the frightful condition of his own soul in the previous episode but also of the possibility of heroic action later. When he rejects Delilah's love, with contemptuous quotation—

'But Love constrained thee'—call it furious rage
To satisfy thy lust: (836)

—he makes an accurate distinction between her jealous anxiety to 'enjoy thee day and night Mine and Loves prisoner' (807), and true love which 'seeks to have Love' rather than to possess the beloved like property.

Delilah (806 ff.) has already hinted at the sexual delights which Samson enjoyed so much; now she offers them again as a bribe for his forgiveness (909) and a recompense for blindness, lasciviously wheedling:

though sight be lost,
Life yet hath many solaces, enjoy'd
Where other senses want not their delights

At home in leisure and domestic ease
Exempt from many a care and chance to which
Eye-sight exposes daily men abroad. (914)

It is an appallingly ironic, insensitive dismissal of what Samson has already felt—the exposure of being blind, 'still as a fool, In power of
others'; the identification of sight with delight; mental pain, and the
failure of all his 'genial powers'; and, above all, the loss of inner vision.
Delilah's simple selfishness condemns her, and she throws away her case
by a final relativism: if Samson will not forgive her, she will enjoy her
triumph—

I shall be nam'd among the famousest
Of Women, sung at solemn festivals . . . (982)

In fact, she was to become notorious, the type of treacherous wifehood,
throughout the Middle Ages and Renaissance, while Samson is being
celebrated 'in copious Legend, or sweet Lyric Song' (1737). But for the
reader there is a further, more equivocal irony: Delilah's last speech
shows her to be so unreliable that Samson's treatment of her is justified
and his vulnerability to her in the past excused; yet Delilah ranges herself
with the Jewish and subsequently Christian heroine 'Jael, who with in-
hospitable guile Smote Sisera sleeping through the Temples nail'd'
(989); and Jael was traditionally ranged with Gideon and Samson.
Probably Milton was handling it with simple-mindedness: even twen-
tieth-century commentators on Judges iv-v see in Jael a model of piety.
A reader not ideologically committed to the story and to Deborah's song
about it might feel that it puts Jael into a more active and political class
than Delilah, but not one entirely different. And what of the third
heroine in these legends, Rahab the prostitute of Jericho, who betrayed
her own city by concealing the Israelite spies, in return for the safety of
her family, for she feared the rumoured invincibility of Israel (Joshua ii,
vi. 25)—was she traitor or good woman? In Hebrews she is listed with
Gideon, Barak, Samson and Jephthah as one who had faith in God. One
of the difficulties of dramatising—hence having to make ethical analyses
of—Christian myth is that so much of it is national. The scholars com-
menting on the Bible saw Jael as a heroine, Rahab an ante-type of Mary
Magdalene, but Delilah a sinner. Of course, there is no excuse for Delilah: she is an intimate traitor. But this prejudicially black-and-white
mythology is less realistic than the Greek. Agamemnon sacrifices his
daughter for the public good; his wife Clytemnestra murders him in re-

venge; but Aeschylus did not leave it there: their son Orestes murders Clytemnestra in her turn; pursued by the Furies, avengers of family blood, he is saved only by a compromise between the blind Furies and rational civic equity.

3rd Stasimon (1010–1060)

There have always been phases of strong anti-feminism or 'masculine protest', usually related to rather strident father-God religious ideals. Donne can mock women horribly:

> Hope not for minde in women; at their best
> Sweetnesse and wit, they'are but *Mummy*, possest.

Yet it is more usual for him to see them as co-agents of peace, happiness and purity:

> If, as I have, you also doe
> Vertue' attir'd in woman see,
> And dare love that, and say so too,
> And forget the Hee and Shee . . .
>
> (*The Undertaking*)

Shakespeare's most fatal women are pitied at the end. Milton tends to revile his. The Chorus here at first are rhythmically flippant—

> But what it is, hard is to say,
> Harder to hit,
> (Which way soever men refer it)

—as though embarrassed, as your Edwardian clubman would be, by the problem of 'the sex'. Then they make a smart rhetorical investigation of it:

> Or was too much of self-love mixt,
> Of constancy no root infixt,
> That either they love nothing, or not long?

So far as this, with its helplessly querulous lilt, represents men's common dismay at women's behaviour, it is dramatic and amusing. But the next strophe suggests it is meant more positively, and more generally, therefore crudely:

> What e're it be, to wisest men and best
> Seeming at first all heavenly under virgin veil,
> Soft, modest, meek, demure,
> Once join'd, the contrary she proves, a thorn
> Intestin, far within defensive arms

> A cleaving mischief, in his way to vertue
> Adverse and turbulent, or by her charms
> Draws him awry enslav'd
> With dotage, and his sense deprav'd
> To folly and shameful deeds which ruin ends.

The phrasing is acute—'A cleaving mischief', 'Draws him awry en-
slav'd With Dotage'; but as an intellectual generalisation it is nonsense.
The rhetorical persuasive formality of argument is akin to the phrasing's
talent, a talent for gaining assent to what is said rather than to the truth
of the matter: the Chorus do not, for instance, question the quality of
that wisdom which in 'wisest men' allows them to be deceived in their
marriage choice.

We have noticed how the maritime imagery, of Delilah 'Like a
stately Ship', presents her as a false breath of air. It is also related to
Samson's own imagery of the 'foolish Pilot' who has 'shipwrack't My
Vessel trusted to me from above, Gloriously rigg'd' (198) because 'Em-
barqu'd with such a Stearsmate at the Helm' (1045). Maritime imagery
for bad subjects was traditional (it is especially strong in the Bible, the
Jews, as opposed to the Phoenicians of Tyre and Sidon, being landsmen).
Milton's frequent use of it represents, though, his horror of the limitless
and unmanageable—of, we should say these days, the unconscious.
There is also, of course, a train of soul-ship imagery, some with the
super-ego in command, others—ships of fools—with youth at the prow
and pleasure at the helm; and we know the ship of death, with the
Woman and her mate Death, in the *Ancient Mariner* (a poem which re-
counts a sin punished with aridity, impotence and loneliness, redeemed
at last by spiritual grace—'But soon there breathed a wind on me, Nor
sound nor motion made').

4th Episode: Samson and Haraphah (1061-1267)

Now the Chorus see another storm different from 'The sumptuous
Dálilah floating this way' (1072). It is Haraphah. He is presented as the
gigantic bully of fairy-tale and school-yarn—a cowardly braggart. This
sets Samson off as a giant of superior kind, and allows him to express a
favourite theme of Milton's, the vanity of martial glory compared with
single-minded virtue:

> Then put on all thy gorgeous arms, thy Helmet
> And Brigandine of brass, thy broad Habergeon ... (1119)

The structure of the play begins to tighten, for this contempt echoes the first chorus celebrating Samson who 'weaponless himself, Made Arms ridiculous' (130). It is confirmed as a sign of renewing strength in Samson's next speech, when he rejects the charge of magic by challenging Haraphah to single combat, each as champion of his god: he is returning to his original role, realising what he had said to Manoah (using the same imagery of medieval tourney, line 463), 'all the contést is now 'Twixt God and *Dagon*'; realising also, in 'champion', one of the senses of *agonistes*. Haraphah then, for the first time in the play, makes objective and so heals Samson's internal despair:

> Presume not on thy God, what e're he be,
> Thee he regards not, owns not, hath cut off . . . (1156)

This evokes from Samson his first expression of hope: 'these evils I deserve and more . . . yet'—he no longer dwells on either evils or guilt—'yet despair not of his final pardon'. Now Haraphah shifts away from Samson's challenge to accuse him of having been merely a privateer, a brutal and capricious Robin Hood. Samson's answer—'I was no private but a person rais'd . . . from Heav'n To free my Countrey' (1211)—evades by mere assertion and contradiction the complicated issues raised even by political, let alone religious, resistance movements. But in the play it effects another advance, for now Samson asserts what so far he has only queried—'O wherefore was my birth from Heaven foretold . . .?' (23). He has recovered faith in God's disposition of his strength; Haraphah retreats; and at once, accruing with faith, is a sudden accession to Samson's strength of the practical wisdom he had lacked in the past: the Chorus fear what Haraphah will do, but Samson, speaking (it is typical of his language in this episode) with crisp sense, argues that he won't dare do anything (1253 ff.).

4th Stasimon (1268–1296)

To this the Chorus respond with the poem's supreme stasimon, a hymn slowly narrowing down from relaxed embracing generality of joy to the local action of the last episode where the Officer enters. Of course there are intellectual objections, as to the Old Testament notion of the hero who 'executes His errand on the wicked'; but they don't make themselves heard against the triumphant rhythms—and it is right that they shouldn't. This strophe celebrates what is properly (though only partially and temporarily) a feeling of subjugate, invaded, persecuted people, that they *are* right and that at last omnipotence is going to join their side.

'But patience is more oft the exercise Of Saints': it is always difficult to distinguish from obdurate stoicism the

> lifetime's death in love,
> Ardour and selflessness and self-surrender

of the Christian saint, especially as the Roman virtues of individual enterprise, rationality and toughness were dearer to Milton than the 'Catholic' virtues that Eliot refers to. Indeed, Milton really doesn't make the distinction in Christian terms at all and, though it is a pre-Christian fable, he should, for if Samson is an ante-type of Christ, this is his Gethsemane. 'Making them each his own Deliverer' (1289) ignores the Christian doctrine that no man is saved (Biblical deliverer = saviour) but by grace. Milton is asserting what had long been for him temperamental axioms: that 'they also serve who only stand and wait'; that public defeat need not obviate private victory; indeed private must precede public victory:

> Yet he who reigns within himself, and rules
> Passions, Desires, and Fears, is more a King;
> Which every wise and vertuous man attains:
> And who attains not, ill aspires to rule
> Cities of men, or head-strong Multitudes,
> Subject himself to Anarchy within,
> Or lawless passions in him which he serves.
>
> (*P.R.* II. 466)

Samson, now winning his private victory over accidie, despair and fallacious comforts, is fitting himself for the public role which he entered the play to escape: the 'unfrequented place' of the parode has filled with tempters and the public voice of the Chorus; and, as they now say, his holiday 'hath bin to thee no day of rest, Labouring thy mind More then the working day thy hands' (1298). It is here in the mechanics of the plot that grace is implied: Samson, relieved by the idolatrous festival which he himself has caused from the drudgery which alone will callouse his soul to its guilt, seeks private ease for his body and finds instead an increasingly public anguish for his mind; but in that anguish finds that all begins to ease.

5th Episode: Samson and Officer (1297–1426)

The Officer who now arrives is the play's most public figure. Samson's reasons for refusing to play before the Philistines come fast: his religion forbids it; then, why should they 'make a game of my calamities' (1331)—a sour comment on the sort of play that might have been written about him; but its tone is noticeably firmer than when he had so feared the mockery or the pity of public gaze. 'Regard thy self, this will offend them highly,' says the kindly Officer, ranging himself almost with Samson, as underdog to 'them'. 'My self? my conscience and internal peace!' Here Samson's dislocated personality comes back into focus. At the beginning of the action he found himself his own sepulchre, annihilated like Donne in *St. Lucy's Day*. The Chorus and Manoah saw him from outside so changed that he seemed to them also to have lost his identity: 'Can this be he?' (124), 'Is this the man?' (340). Then Samson had hugged in guilt and made of that, and secluded drudgery, and coming death, a sort of person, but one having no relation either to God or the self he had been. But though his feelings then had no value, his confession—'I my self have brought them on, Sole Author I, sole cause' (375)—as it were cast out that dead husk into the ground so there really was nothing left inside; then, tilled by Delilah and Haraphah and now the Officer, the seed has rooted in faith and grown into a new identity. It is no longer concerned about itself in the former sense of a mortified organism, quelled, blind, capable only of sensating anguish; it is differentiated into a palpable objective being, and an internal conscientious self; yet integrated into the total wilful 'I' of 'I will not come' (1342). The accession of grace and strength is indicated casually, but it is apparent in the way Samson speaks. It is now he who reassures the Chorus, with rhythms which are actually brisk—

> Besides, how vile, contemptible, ridiculous,
> What act more execrably unclean, prophane? (1361)

He had lowered his neck to the shame of being 'ridiculous, despoil'd, Shav'n, and disarm'd among my enemies' (539); now he sees even that objectively, and with indignation (which implies dignity) for himself and for God. Then he justifies himself (to Milton's audience, learned in the subtleties of legality and sin), claiming again God's right to 'dispense with me or thee Present in Temples at Idolatrous Rites For some important cause' (1377); he asserts the freedom of his will; and suddenly, impelled by 'rouzing motions', decides to go with the Officer. There is a last flicker of his fear of shame, but it is expressed with proper dignity—'Because they shall not trail me through thir streets like a wild Beast, I am content to go' (1402); and then for the Officer a sly acknowledgment of ordinary, unheroic motive which makes obvious to us that he has transcended it:

> Masters commands come with a power resistless
> To such as owe them absolute subjection;
> And for a life who will not change his purpose?
> (So mutable are all the ways of men)

The irony is complicated: his purpose has never been other than to relinquish life; what has changed is the mood in which he goes to meet death. To Manoah he refused life out of despair; to Delilah, out of knowledge and singlemindedness; to Haraphah he defied death out of pride; now he meets 'oft-invocated death' not as 'the welcome end of all my pains' (575), the ease he had sought in the parode, but as the willed end, the goal, of a revived personality.

5th Stasimon (1427–1440)

The Chorus's benediction—'Go, and the Holy One Of *Israel* be thy guide' (1427)—takes up a number of psalms and perhaps especially this passage from *Isaiah*:

> Fear thou not; for I am with thee . . . they that strive with thee shall perish . . . For I the Lord thy God will hold thy right hand, saying unto thee, Fear not; I will help thee . . . I will help thee, saith the Lord, and thy redeemer, the Holy One of Israel. (xli. 10–14)

The Chorus turn the angel that foretold Samson's birth into a guardian angel, and the spirit of his strength into the Holy Spirit. The cadence of their blessing, with its final rhyme, at lines 1438–40, dismisses Samson from the ordinary world.

Exode (1441–1659)

At once, though, Manoah comes to take Samson home to that world. He hurriedly tells his good news, its private success interrupted by the two great public noises, of the Philistines 'shouting to behold Thir once great dread, captive and blind before them' (1473), and of the temple's crash 'As if the whole inhabitation perish'd' (1512). Manoah and the

Chorus fluster between hopes and fears, still closed in their personal interests. The Messenger (who in Greek tragedy must always tell of the violence not permitted on stage) arrives, but there is further forced quibbling suspense. When at last it is made clear that Samson is dead, Manoah utters a curious speech:

> The worst indeed, O all my hope's defeated
> To free him hence! but death who sets all free
> Hath paid his ransom now and full discharge.
> What windy joy this day I had conceiv'd
> Hopeful of his Delivery, which now proves
> Abortive as the first-born bloom of spring
> Nipt with the lagging rear of winters frost. (1571)

The first line and a half tie the speech into Manoah's actions so far; but then he changes to a rhythm and use of active personifying metaphor which is Shakespearean. His 'windy joy' is akin to Delilah's false breeze; and the sharp modulation puts Manoah's feeble efforts at material ransom behind him, and compresses his suffering for his son's death into a little tragedy of his own; then the subsequent fully Miltonic, highly syntactical lines, steady him for an understanding of the whole action:

> Yet e're I give the rains to grief, say first,
> How dy'd he? death to life is crown or shame.
> All by him fell thou say'st, by whom fell he,
> What glorious hand gave *Samson* his deaths wound?

The Messenger's story releases the audience by projecting into mimed physical action Samson's earlier convulsions of soul: that is, the end and the release occur externally to Samson, rather than, as we feel they do for Shakespeare's heroes, however historical, 'organically', as if from inner compulsion. Similarly, the motive for his end, and its value, appear not so much in the action as in the celebration of them by the second semichorus. The extraordinary images, of phoenix, snake and eagle, do not represent Samson but the 'vertue' he embodies—ethical goodness, bodily strength and spiritual virility. Here, more Shakespearean lines enact what they celebrate: the 'rouzing motions' are identified with the phoenix, an emblem of Christ's resurrection: they bring him to life again, transcending blindness and contempt; then he comes like a snake along the ground into the home of the unsuspecting and now themselves ridiculous domestic birds of Gaza; but it is as an eagle, born of Zeus, emblem of victory and sovereignty, that his power bolts on them from above, in sign of being not his but God's.

Kommos (1660–1758)

Manoah's last speech, and the final Chorus, read more like critical comments making the best of the play, than expressions of sentiment within it. Manoah insists twice that 'Nothing is here for tears'; he feels his own family made famous out of shame; he sees that Samson has regained his identity, 'hath quit himself/Like *Samson*'; and he plans a cult to keep the fame alive. Yet his last words, about the virgins who shall strew Samson's tomb 'Only bewailing His lot unfortunate in nuptial choice, From whence captivity and loss of eyes', are either the expression of an old bereaved father's *idée fixe*, in which case they are amusing in a 'character-part' way inappropriate to this phase; or they are a public invitation to regard the play as the tragedy of a mistaken marriage, in which case much of what has gone before loses its spiritual significance. It is another of those curious *naïvétes* of Milton, which the eighteenth-century reader recognised with less sympathy but more common sense than we (conditioned to revere Milton as 'great literature' and from a further distance of time) do. The eighteenth-century editor Bishop Newton introduced the Samson myth as 'but a very indifferent one for a dramatic fable. However, he has made the best of it. He seems to have chosen it for the sake of the satire on bad wives.'

We must not allow the final chorus to entangle us in a discussion of what exactly Aristotle meant by the purgation of pity and terror. Again, they are commending the play as a conventional tragedy rather than acting in it to produce in us the condition they commend. We may note two things, though. Firstly, 'calm of mind all passion spent' has the tone of statement, almost epigram. The 'calm' and 'spent' do not suggest the exhausted serenity that one finds at the end of *Sohrab and Rustum*, for example. It is still firm, rational, even curt, a conventional gesture which dismisses the audience from the poem. This gesture derives, secondly, from the emphatic complex of words, dispose–intent–event–dismist. With these, the Chorus aver faith. It is not the individual spiritual faith of Dante and Eliot and the mystics, a faith identified with love in which the human will rests, unanxious about its own motives and worthiness, in the will of God. It is based on Paul's assurance, 'we know that all things work together for good to them that love God, to them who are the called according to His purpose' (*Rom.* viii. 28). But the ode's tight form—almost an octosyllabic sonnet—and the cool latinate keywords present it as a faith more intellectual, mechanical and cosmic—in fact, Augustan. The image of God as a clouded sun, which 'unexpectedly returns' to shed its glory on the eclipsed sun-god Samson, faintly suggests the mystic's apprehension; but the abstract effect of 'dispose' and 'intent' is dominant; it implies a faith based on demonstration clear as geometry of God's beneficent power to consult on and resolve 'the sum of things' (*P.L.* VI. 673).

It is appropriate to this work. Where more naturalistic art invites us to reside almost lovingly within it, Milton excludes us most of the time from empathetic participation: we stand back from it to contemplate and, without much personal feeling, admire. In order to realise, to take in to ourselves, much of what is being done in the play and even in the details of its language, we have to bring to it a good deal of information; for Milton, as we noticed at the beginning, does not usually 'create' the feelings or the things he is writing about, but rather takes them as given and abstracts from them intellectual summaries or patterns. For example, on the small scale, in the local language, we have a series of gibes at various kinds of falsity: 'the forgery Of brazen shield and spear' (131)—that is, of romantic might—related to 'How counterfeit a coin they are who friends Bear in their Superscription' (189) and so to the 'fair fallacious looks, venereal trains' (533) of Delilah, which are also the 'fair enchanted cup, and warbling charms' (934) of Circe, who turned men into beasts, and the 'snares' of church and state which Delilah says she was caught in (845). Locally they seem repetitive and either trite or punningly persuasive ('forgery' punningly asserts that romantic might is false; Shakespeare's major puns, like 'honest' and 'fool', analyse the nature of honesty and folly with a dramatic dialectic). Over the whole poem, though, they spread a network (rather brittle) of deceitful complications, which—and this is where we move to the larger scale of the action—can be got out of only by faithful commitment to a single believed-in 'right'. That is symbolised by Samson's last single prayerful act which demonstrates the fallacy of Dagon-worship, breaks out of Delilah's snare and destroys the chivalric 'choice nobility and flower' of Philistia.

3. Conclusion

The title of *Samson Agonistes* refers to the sense of champion or protagonist as well as athlete. But, in spite of the exaltation of some of the choruses, the dominant echo is of Laocoönian agony. It is patterned into a spiritual development; it is cast in the mould of a strict authority which becomes at the end actual paternal care for the forgiven son; but these are not enough. There is not enough context of character, scene, event, language, to absorb the cries of anguish: they are too starkly uttered individual *words*—'O dark, dark, dark'. The words are propelled by irresistible rhythms:

> But thee whose strength, while vertue was her mate,
> Might have subdu'd the Earth,
> Universally crown'd with highest praises. (173)

> So deal not with this once thy glorious Champion,
> The Image of thy strength, and mighty minister. (705)

>   bulk without spirit vast,

> .   .   .

> Stalking with less unconsci'nable strides,
> And lower looks, but in a sultrie chafe. (1238)

But they are not harmonised. The verse in general typifies Samson's career and the old-fashioned theory of tragedy, hurling up sharp notes, quick hard words and then dejecting them:

> By how much from the top of wondrous glory,
> Strongest of mortal men,
> To lowest pitch of abject fortune thou art fall'n. (167)

Falling rhythms are natural in English (though rare in *Comus*). But even when the sense is positive—

> Assailant on the perchèd roosts,
> And nests in order rang'd
> Of tame villatic Fowl (1693)

—it is the force of single words or phrases that counts, not the collected power of paragraph or ode. All the lines in the poem tend to the word-by-word vibration of Samson's final act—'He tugged/he shook/

till down/ they came/ and drew/ the whole roof after them' (1650). It is
natural that language should be impressive in lament or violence, but
everywhere in *Samson* it impresses blow by blow, whether refined to
abstraction—'Effeminatly vanquish't' (562)—or harshly colloquial—
'avoided as a blab' (495). And there is not so much a tension or reciproca-
tion between these different orders of diction, as mutual contempt:
'trivial weapon' (263), 'sedentary numness' (571), 'Mangle my appre-
hensive tenderest parts' (624), 'With malediction mention'd, and the
blot Of falshood most unconjugal traduc't' (978), 'A secular bird ages or
lives' (1707). These are detailed examples of that clash between authority
and personality discussed in the Introduction. Another set is the recur-
rence of contradictories—strength and weakness, physical and spiritual
virtue, siege, shipwreck, stings, light and dark, selfhood and shame.
There is no reconciliation, only an end: 'now all labour Mars what it
does; yea, very force entangles Itself with strength' (*Antony*, IV. xiv. 47).

This uncompromising discordant finality seems, as a whole, a fruitless
exercise of repressed talent. It is difficult to judge because of the form's
authority and the expression's eccentricity; the best we can do is to put
it against those passages in *Four Quartets* where T. S. Eliot (quoting 'O
dark dark dark' in *East Coker* and alluding to Milton in *Little Gidding* as
'one who died blind and quiet') analyses the pains of talent, motive and
old age.

Select Bibliography

Annotated Texts

G. and M. Bullough, ed. *Milton's Dramatic Poems* (University of Athlone Press, 1958). Excellent.

A. W. Verity, ed. *Comus* and *Samson Agonistes* (Cambridge University Press, 1909, 1892, respectively). Fussy.

M. Y. Hughes, ed. *Paradise Regained, The Minor Poems and Samson Agonistes* (The Odyssey Press, New York, 1937). More expensive but very good, with a sister-volume for *Paradise Lost*.

Comus—Criticism

G. Wilson Knight, 'The Frozen Labyrinth, An Essay on Milton' in his *The Burning Oracle* (Oxford University Press, 1939). An impressionistic account.

R. M. Adams, 'Reading *Comus*' in his *Ikon: John Milton and the Modern Critics* (Cornell University Press, 1955). Attacks the major scholarly interpretations.

Comus—Related Reading

Works referred to in this book.

Marvell, 'A Dialogue between the Resolved Soul and Created Pleasure'.

Blake, 'Nurse's Song' and 'Night' in *Songs of Innocence*; 'Nurse's Song', 'The Little Girl Lost' and 'The Little Girl Found' in *Songs of Experience*.

Edgar Windt, *Pagan Mysteries of the Renaissance* (for the Three Graces, etc.).

Blake did some illustrations to *Comus*; the best paintings to look at in relation to the poem are Botticelli's.

Samson Agonistes—Criticism

F. M. Krouse, *Milton's Samson and the Christian Tradition* (Princeton University Press, 1949).

Arnold Stein, *Heroic Knowledge: an Interpretation of 'Paradise Regained' and 'Samson Agonistes'* (University of Minneapolis Press, 1957). This essay owes a good deal to it.

Samson Agonistes—Related Reading

Works referred to in this book.

T. S. Eliot, 'A Dialogue on Dramatic Poetry' in his *Selected Essays*; *Murder in the Cathedral*; *Four Quartets*.

Rembrandt's 1628 painting of Samson shorn and being seized (Berlin) is helpful.